THE SECOND PERFECT NUMBER

poems by

Joanna Solfrian

Finishing Line Press
Georgetown, Kentucky

THE SECOND
PERFECT NUMBER

ACKNOWLEDGMENTS

Grateful acknowledgment is made to Matthew Lippman, editor of
www.lovesexecutiveorder.com, where "Trump-Era Commute" was originally
published; also to Shane McCrae and Image, which published "Pops,
Independence Day" under the title "Pops."

Thank you also to the February Poem-A-Day group for reading these poems
in their original form. You make the longest month the richest.

Publisher: Leah Huete de Maines
Editor: Christen Kincaid
Cover Design: Peter Miles, petermilesstudio.com
Author Photo: David P. Squid Quinn

Order online: www.finishinglinepress.com
also available on amazon.com

Author inquiries and mail orders:
Finishing Line Press
PO Box 1626
Georgetown, Kentucky 40324
USA

Table of Contents

[A perfect number is] a positive integer that is equal to the sum of its proper divisors. The smallest perfect number is 6, which is the sum of 1, 2, and 3...The discovery of such numbers is lost in prehistory. It is known, however, that the Pythagoreans (founded c. 525 BCE) studied perfect numbers for their "mystical" properties.

– Encyclopedia Britannica

Eat not the heart.

– Pythagorean maxim

for Olive and Willa

Convince Me That the World Is Right
February 1st

Once more my heart has pains.
I pray my pen will order my sorrows.

This morning, the children gathered around their stories,
and with coffee cups the parents bent for the infinite.

I've used my tongue to taste words, their bitter nail and velvet.
The ones that speak of love taste like your tongue.

Why does the mist I elect most often keep me from awe?
I am silent for the sake of sidewalks, their mute servitude.

This morning the children read their stories.
A secondary god blessed their sober, gleaming heads.

New York Super Fudge Chunk
February 2nd

Yesterday the Hudson froze. On the deli tv, Darío and I watched
the shattered floes before he spied a line and rang me up.

Today, Saturday: children, and I their mother. The day will run
away on their feet: cartoons, groceries, playdates.

This morning, morning came. The sun bled out over night's
tender stars, and the squirrel out my window got on with it.

In case all this gets convivial, I've stashed loneliness in my back pocket!
I knew what I was getting. I signed the form when I was born.

It is my habit to tiptoe towards love so that my footprints
resemble moons. No idol comes close to that kind of god.

A Mighty Fortress
February 3rd

Last night we lit our eyes and our lips became moons from the gaze.
The wine bottle envied how you decanted into me.

Sundays too I used to be at church, an amateur lover
hunting God in the wine that trembled in the thimble-glasses.

The cat is curled at my hip. His griefs do not measure
the same as mine, and our relationship is somewhat formal.

Some thoughts electrocute, like sleep to the insomniac.
Buried in these words are instructions for weeping.

If I die early, you insist you won't remarry. Do!
As it is, the newspapers tell of too much sorrow.

(from Fare & Folk window)
February 4th

In front of the elementary school, exhaust floats from a minivan.
I look down to my notebook, then up: another minivan.

Seers read secrets in the constellations of leaves.
Which hunter, which sister will be at the bottom of my cup?

I knew a man who came home from a two-month hospital stay.
He rolled to the window, found his favorite cardinal and waved goodbye.

People say there is a veil between the living and the dead.
If this is true, Jo, you should make more attempts.

4:28 a.m.
February 5th

When I share my bed with my beloved, I must remember
that the libretto to love is snoring.

In my dream I asked him, *would you like to listen to a big toe?*
then guided his hand to my belly. *Should we tell the kids?*

I am seized by love, divisionless Being.
This is the perfect number, though I keep talking!

If you want to hear sounds of the old century, listen
to the river. Or to the children's shell-ears when they sleep.

No wonder you came looking for me: you,
the writer of melodies, and I a desperate violin.

Fare & Folk
February 6th

Without thought I woke and put on your diamond.
Later that day, a student called to say *her* mother would die.

I still have the power of sight, though I've split open twice.
Last night I kissed their brows, then my pen ran out of ink.

Men have split mountains for the sake of a diamond.
For what sake does a mother die?

At the coffee shop this morning, I ran into friends twice.
One bejeweled, the other as bald as an old pot of ink.

Lightning illuminates as it falls. When ink
falls at daybreak, the sky's diamonds die twice.

Trump-Era Commute
February 7th

The construction worker steps aside on the sidewalk.
(Eastern European?) *Excuse me, lady. Good morning, lady!*

Last night in the subway, a loon, unhinged, unmedicated:
Look at you, man, fuck you, you're ugly. Aw, man, I'm sorry. Fuck you.

Today, in the face across from me, an aspect of the dead writer.
As he reads his book, I gape at the bend of his eyebrows.

The MTA tape loops: *Hello! It's dangerous to hold the doors open.*
Hello! It's dangerous to hold the doors open. Hello! It's dangerous—

If you've retained any degree of hope, you must be hallucinating.
The apples in the garden are not apples but visions of apples.

Van Vorhees Park
February 8th

Today was a difficult day to be human. After misunderstood words,
I saw the high-dangling chestnut burrs, and longed for their view.

The best days are the days I lose my reason.
Courting the lunatic, I pour another glass.

I woke this morning, yanked from a dream. Who cares?
I'm most interested in the yanking.

Letters keep arriving in pastels. "We're sorry for your loss"
the winner, easily beating out "we loved him."

Every child understands the omnipresence of love.
When my child was one, "I love you" was just "I you."

On Re-Reading Christian Wiman's *My Bright Abyss: Meditation of a Modern Believer*
February 9th

Saturday: sleepovers, birthday party. Paper-plated pizza slices,
the moronic sorority of mothers in a clutch.

I judge too much, lob pyrotechnics from my brain,
then self-flagellate with the nearest pool noodle.

I don't want heaven to be elsewhere, all-healing. I want to die
into life, so I can repair my relationship with paper plates.

"Quantum weirdness": the unobserved particle
goes through multiple screen-holes, the observed only one.

What I observe of mothers, parties, the cat now grooming its anus
is altered by my means of perception. This feels like bad news.

Yes, all religion is an attempt to comprehend the numinous.
Careful, Jo: as your pen drains, so does the divine.

Monkey Bars
February 10th

From its clear home the wind watched my child
and remembered what it had been—alive! alive!—

do I dare view my soul from the outside?
How is such a thing possible?

My madness is competence.
If we meet and you deem me well-spoken, help.

When piano notes rise, they alter the shape of air.
My soul weaves its gown from those shapes.

At night, my child discloses her life to me.
When we cuddle, she still makes of her thumb a nipple.

Definitions
February 11th

Ego: bringing God down to my human stance
by writing lines that pretend to know something of God.

A means to eternity: the poem, hah hah!
Only if the self does not author it.

Adolescence: my older child, kind, forbearing,
whacks her sister upside the head.

Ecstasy: the dead soul star bangs a piano
and licks heaven's floor with his falsetto.

And what of midlife? Our conversation lasted the bottle.
When we got to the dregs, we were still old friends.

Married, Middle-Aged
February 12th

The trees speak their language of wars and songs.
When we meet in the garden, we listen.

Come wash in the rapid dress of the brook.
The stone loves the water's plumes, and you.

The new pains travel the sorrows of my hands
which travel the sorrows of your hands.

Would you have heard the stairs age as I crept to the belfry?
I was seven. My sandals released dust from its gravity.

Now, my uterus gathers roads, wounds, whole cities I've never seen.
In two days' time it will evict them all.

St. Paul's, Court Street
February 13th

I sneak into the transept, where light enrobes your mortal name.
This is my argument against mountains, the iron votive stand.

Only in the solitude of dying hours do I hear life calling to me.
My friend, this is normally when I try to say something wise.

Though the poverty of my imagination allows for no boats,
I see a small skiff, waiting, like a patient in a white gown.

I don't know whether it's true that the locus of rapture
is the gap between deed and love. That was something I wrote.

Later today, I will take the subway to my office. Magnetic, expansive
    life:
I succumb to your sparrows, your clumps of snow.

Feb. 14th
February 14th

On your skin, the salty taste of spindrift. You make
of your mouth a tunnel, and birds fly to it—I fly to it.

Your body makes of the world an actuality of mountains.
In sleep I cleave to you, a thin line of shale.

As the clock slices time into rounds, I suffer the invasion of thought.
Then morning comes, and infinitesimal armies ditch camp.

I wake early to the sound of a bell.
My child in the next room, laughing with the kitty.

My children, all I want is to hold you, bury my face in your necks,
exhale whole roads that you may or may not follow.

It is the day of love. St. Valentine in his cell writes words
in blood, lures a sparrow to fly them home.

Plane

February 15th

I have travelled far today with my children and beloved.
It is warm where we are. They sleep.

Some days you have to leave the vastness of the city
to carry within your own halls the vastness of thought.

It is strange to have no parents. "I can do whatever I want,"
I said to my children, then loaded the dishwasher.

Everywhere I go, centuries trail my feet.
Dusk: equatorial ancestors who belong to other beings.

There is no money here for food. At the market,
the man in line before me bought a loaf, a tin.

Jo, why so conflicted?
In the nave, prayers already sleep in books.

Coral Bay, St. John
February 16th

What are you writing? the bartender (tanned, friendly) asks me.
I'm translating a poem from the Spanish. He stops mid-pour; considers.

No one can speak until they speak of the hurricanes.
The lady next to me says *I lost everything*, then turns to the now-quiet bay.

I tell the children that "maho" means heart, or love,
I can't remember which. *Taíno? They died out.*

Tomorrow we'll walk the ruins of the enslaved. The lady and I do a shot.
Her house—the first time the word has come to mind aptly—*smithereens*.

This island is full of ghosts. *Jumbies.* My children,
wiser than I, believe—and after dark will not set foot outside.

Pops, Independence Day
February 17th

I remember you in your final atonement, how calm you were.
Though you couldn't tell me, you understood the names hidden in the
    dusk.

I wish I could've given you my arms, so that you'd have recognized
a tether to earth, but in your stupor you needed to forget things.

I wonder sometimes about the work of your eyes.
What did they see in the ceiling that made the nurse clutch her breast?

You felt no injury over the climateless beeps and drips.
I do the crossword by your side: per aspera ad _____.

Then out the plate glass, mute: fireworks.
And for two, maybe three seconds, they drape the sky with jewels.

As a human, you were nearly blameless. You won't let go
of the bouquet I picked from the courtyard, until it is time to let go.

4.1

February 18th

At times, marriage means adapting to erosions. The film tonight
involved a sinking ship, and the house we're staying in wiggled.

"Wiggled" is a funny word, but that's what tonight's earthquake did.
This morning we passed a makeshift dump for hurricane debris.

My belief in God needs to adapt to its own erosions.
Post-9/11, every subway malfunction incinerated the riders' eyes.

I get it. If not tectonics or climate change, assholes. *I need a minute.*
There's a bird's nest in a pew of the roofless Moravian church.

Jo, stop thinking of the soul as nebulous.
It is a knife, and the sea into which the knife disappears.

The Very Craving Does Not Give It Back to Us
February 19th

When you left, you gave your name to the mortal winds.
It was time to become a stranger to ratiocination.

I'm simply trying to record my existence!
After one blank page, another blank page.

Yesterday, a sudden, cooling rain: a vendor tarped a calabash.
She comes, she leaves—the vendor sucked her teeth—*the sky can't make
   up her mind.*

As a teen, my father mowed the cemetery. In the records' room: "Baby
   Marsden."
"That was your brother," his mother said over three-bean sandwiches.

For now, death is a mere theme—
but we don't know, we don't know.

Only Once a Vision Came to Me
February 20th

Only once a vision came to me. A blue-gold fish suspended
without agent, nearly from floor to ceiling,

at the foot of my bed. *Look, look*—I elbowed
the husband-mound, but he slept, and I remained mute.

The giant fish opened and closed its mouth. Each scale shot
light. It rotated a few degrees left, a few right. I sat, bolt-

upright the glorious glow. Yes! I am awake! I am happy!
Then—somehow—morning.

I scraped open from sleep and saw the gray sheets,
the feeble sun. And as you have sensed,

I spent the day in sober thought
and am only speaking of this now.

(on what would've been your 77th birthday)
February 21st

I am writing about today
so you can come with me

the green balloons of thought
do they ever arrive

this morning I swam
with the children

mom I have children
I just tidied the moon

off the floor and tossed
it back to the sky

the itinerant clouds
don't look back

where are you these
twenty-five years?

Travel

February 22nd

Night comes slowly to our hands,
the blue night that wanders alone over the world.

Out my window, a fête of stars and myths.
I like to cup them in my hands and press them to my face.

Tonight for dinner, the last onion, the last slices of bread.
As ever, my agony is love.

Soon, where will we go? What words will we speak?
The children will return to school, to slights real and imagined.

I wish for them the liberty of dusk,
how it erases what is vegetation, what is human…

The Reflexive Property
February 23rd

You are mine as much as anyone can be mine.
Every time I see you, my thoughts arrest.

Your solitude is my solitude:
this is why there's so much joy.

Whatever song I've buried waits for you to tread kindly by.
On the page I hoard the moon. No shit, I'm a fool.

I make my mother-boast when I spy you sleeping:
aw, that elbow—I grew that.

The "you" is anyone who wants it—
skin's a shield for blood, bone: not identity.

Return

February 24th

In the shape of a trumpet my voice has come to my body,
the way love comes to the sidewalk in the form of weeds.

Tonight, gusts of winds shuddered and pitched the plane.
The woman in the seat behind me laughed, teeth like artillery.

All this polarity thinking has got us nuts. *You're either with us or—*
where's the wonder? The daffodil spires are both choir and judge.

(Under my thigh I release the spit valve,
and onto the floor drop three small speeches.)

I haven't read the news in two weeks.
That angel we called—did she come?

Prayer

February 25th

We made you the way God makes stars. Then the doctor dug and
    pulled,
and you unplugged, sudden verb. Somewhere a hand wrote your name.

We tiptoe through your dark room to watch your curled form sleep.
You are distant as a planet in its elliptical drift, and we stand, fixed.

You no longer cry out for us. You've grown a trunk, seven layers
inside you. I try to feel them now through your leg, warm on top of
    the blanket—

a twitch. Temporary Death goes, *sprint back*: so I hold on,
a desperate stranger, made eccentric by my role as the one who holds
    on.

Waking From a Dream
February 26th

When I place my feet on the floor all sense of you condenses
into a pebble, which I spend the rest of my day looking for.

There is another kind of waiting which happens in the room
deep inside your being, the one with dust on its chair.

The sea gave up its idea of mirrors long ago.
And we are supposed to know something of the stars, their corridors?

This is all very melancholy because I am melancholy.
Because I am melancholy, that is what I think of this.

When death endeavors to doom I run topless through a cornfield.
The cob stares me down with many eyes, and I laugh.

My Human Condition
February 27th

Each morning my child releases the doves that sleep in her hair.
She wakes early, consults the cat on his evening.

The first spirit got a bum egg and my tube exploded. For fourteen hours
I bled internally, then blacked out to a hand opening the moon.

When I walk to work, I carry the schoolyard's bright cries in my chest.
What is now was a now and will be a now. Fucking quantum physics.

Darling, call in sick. Let's play cards with images of old lovers.
Small deck!

The gutter-drop is happiest when it joins the river.
Today, when I have conversations, I'll look people in the eye.

The Second Perfect Number
February 28th

To receive the marvels one must wait a lot.
For the birdsong, for the train, for the cells to fall in line.

Only once was I brave enough to open the steeple hatch.
The trees rioted with fall; the wind, corpulent mystic, dizzied my head.

The room to which my dead have ascended
is unfamiliar to me. I am horizontal, and dusty.

The human duty is to seek joy! In the park a tutued moon-bellied
girl, maybe four, stops to pick her nose.

My flaw is attempting to record these fugitive moments.
What is your second perfection, my fugitive friend?

Notes

This series was written in the month of a recent February. Two books from that month's reading have influenced it: Christian Wiman's *My Bright Abyss: Meditation of a Modern Believer* and Pablo Neruda's *Twenty Love Poems and a Song of Despair* (translated by W.S. Merwin). A few phrases in these poems come from mistranslations of Neruda's poems; as a poor Spanish speaker, I'm taken in by false cognates. Nonetheless, I'm grateful for the generative errors the poems provided.

"Fare & Folk" is for Nelle Jaffee and Lila Marguiles, "Definitions" is for Tom Bernardo, and "Coral Bay, St. John" is for Christopher Conboy Jr. and George Rendell.

All love poems are for Scott Solfrian.

Joanna Solfrian's first book, *Visible Heavens*, was chosen by Naomi Shihab Nye for the Stan and Tom Wick Poetry Prize, a national first book award. Her poems have appeared in journals such as *The Harvard Review, Boulevard, Rattle, Margie, The Southern Review, Salamander, Pleiades, Image,* and also in the internationally-touring art exhibit *Speak Peace: American Voices Respond to Vietnamese Children's Paintings.* Her second book, *The Mud Room,* was published by MadHat Press. A graduate of the Stonecoast MFA program, she has been nominated for four Pushcart Prizes. Solfrian lives and works in New York City. www.joannasolfrian.com

CPSIA information can be obtained
at www.ICGtesting.com
Printed in the USA
JSHW030804230221
11879JS00005B/18